Peace Poems

and meditations on peace

First published in 2003 by Crocus
Crocus books are published by Commonword Ltd,
6 Mount Street, Manchester M2 5NS.

Crocus books are distributed by Turnaround Publisher
Services Ltd, Unit 3, Olympia Trading Estate, Coburg Road,
Wood Green, London N22 6TZ.

Cover design by Ian Bobb.

Printed by Shanleys, 18 Belvoir Street, Tongue Fold,
Bolton BL2 6BA.

British Library Cataloguing-in-Publication Data. A catalogue
record for this book is available from the British Library.

Contents

Moments: People

Moments: Places

Acknowledgements

Japanese Garden by Muhammad Khalil first published in *And J is For Jazz* (Red Beans and Rice).

The Last Time by Anjum Malik first published in *Before The Rains* (The University Press, Bradford).

Whalley Abbey by Helen Clare first published in *Daily Mirror* 16/1/2001.

Last But One Patrol by David Bateman previously broadcast on *BBC Radio Merseyside.*

Recollections in Tranquility by David Bateman first published in *Curse of The Killer Hedge* (Iron Press 1996).

World To Rights by David Bateman first published in *The Express.*

Too Young To Forget by Philip Burton first published in *Skald,* Issue 11.

Preface

Healthier than a shot of whisky, less of a fire hazard than scented candles, more portable than a flotation tank, *Peace Poems* is a massage for the soul. And in the twenty first century how that massage is needed by us all!

The pace of life has speeded up. It is now a 24 7 12 world. The telephone and fax have been succeeded by mobile phones and texting. Many people are now juggling one, even two jobs, relationships, perhaps family life. And the future has become less certain in all these spheres, as change accelerates.

Peace Poems aims to create that pause, that little gap of sanity and relaxation amid all the haste. It is a collection to be taken after commuter traffic jams, after heated arguments between best friends, at snatched lunch breaks, in dentists' waiting rooms, when the last child is finally put to bed, when the news reports finally end.

The collection is arranged into five loose sections of poems, mixed with meditations from famous people. It is a book to dip into as well as read cover to cover. It features a wide range of styles, because the poems are as diverse and unusual as the people who wrote them.

Peace Poems is a balm and an inspiration for headlong, crazy days. If the saying of the Buddha is true that one peace poem is worth a thousand useless poems, then this collection should go a long way: bringing a sustained cool breeze of calm to your life.

With sincere thanks to co-editors Graeme Kenna and Shamshad Khan.

Pete Kalu

An End To Strife

We must find an alternative to violence. The eye-for-an-eye philosophy leaves everybody blind.

Martin Luther King Jr

Let There Be Peace

Lemn Sissay

Let there be peace
So frowns fly away like albatross
And skeletons fox trot from cupboards
So war correspondents become travel show presenters
And magpies bring back lost property-
Children, engagement rings, broken things

Let there be peace
So storms go out to sea to be angry
And return calm
So the older ones can rise up and dance in the
        hospitals
Let the african man in the block of flats
Peer through his window and see Addis stretched
        out before him
And let the hot sun melt on his face
So his outstretched arms become frames
For his dreams

Let there be peace
Let tears evaporate into clouds, cleanse themselves
And fall into the reservoirs of drinkwater
Let dark memories burst into fireworks that melt
Into the perfect darkness like silver fish in the
        deep sea
And let the waves reach the shore with a
        shhhhhhh, a shhhhhhh, a shhhhhhh

Fending Off The Cold

Philip Davenport

It came out of clear blue
eye-poppingly beautiful morning:

low, night-flying cold
chilling warnings
extraordinary cold propaganda
aircraft carriers in the cold Arabian Sea.

I am fending off the cold
broadcasts said in Pashtu and Dari
I am fending off
cold hands in the air
on brutally
eye-poppingly cold mornings.

Diary

Elizabeth Parish

11.09.01

An ordinary sort of day.

Winds light to moderate,
skies overcast,
but generally fine.

A busy morning:
commuters rattling to the city,
gabbling on their mobiles;
traffic on the street
in stop-start queues;
planes beetle-droning overhead
as usual.

And in the afternoon,

the world changed.

12.09.01

Falling rain.
A little, keening wind.

Pin-drop silence on the train,
no words, no mobiles,
only newsprint, rustling.

Traffic muted.
Unfocused faces,
ashen, gaunt,
gazing out of windows.

Listen.
Flinch.

The echo and shadow of a plane.

World To Rights

David Bateman

After thanking all the world leaders
for attending this meeting
I have called at such short notice,
I explain to them all
in terms simple enough
even for world leaders to understand
exactly how they must work together
to stamp out poverty, injustice,
bigotry and pollution.
The logic of my argument is not only sound
but also incontrovertible and persuasive
and at the end of my speech
there is much shaking of hands, clasping of
        shoulders
and generally wondering why they hadn't already
agreed to this a long time ago,
but when I wake up I can never remember
quite how I phrased it all.

Jean says that sometimes in my sleep
I make noises a bit like words.

The God of peace is never glorified by human violence.

Thomas Merton

When Will There Be Peace?

Graeme Kenna

When the quick death of
Ten thousand white men in suits
Looking to the skies a hundred floors up
Is accounted equal
To the slow death of
Ten thousand black men in rags
Face down in the dust
Then there will be peace

When the last man's grip
Relaxes on the throat of
The second to last man
And he knows that for all
His religion, his race, his language,
He has been as much a man as himself
And he must bear the collective guilt of the age
Then there will be peace

In the silence of the barren world
There will be peace

Imagine

Cathy Bolton

The cab driver has a passing resemblance
to America's most wanted.
His radio's on the blink
so he offers to serenade me – just name my tune.
He did Frank Sinatra for his last fare:
a group of students, pissed up kids
who split themselves all the way to Rusholme.
We're dodging drunks on the A6.
He knows this ambush terrain
like the back streets of the Koran,
dreams of blank faces smeared on the windscreen.
I want to know what he thinks about the war,
ask instead, *What's your favourite song?*
Imagine, he tells me. *I'm living for today.*

takers

copland smith

Alexander, Nero, Caesar
Cortez and Pizarro
 they took the peace

At the Somme, at Mons and Wipers
Amritsar, Wounded Knee
Auschwitz and Masada
 they took the peace

Kings, Queens, Protectors
Presidents, Dictators
Chairmen and Prime Ministers
 all took the peace

Blair, Osama, Dubya
 you're taking the peace

Make Love Not War

Poppy Fitzpatrick

It seemed so simple then
when I was four
slipping pocket money back
into your purse
to purchase peace
Now at forty
I cash in peace of mind
that I tried to
source the route of your anguish

The row would
spin out for days
fed by frustration and
anger but mostly disappointment
that love did not equal peace
for your life

You told me how I
was pushed along the
Aldermaston walk with
a banner carrying
Ban The Bomb
whilst cups flew in the air
at home
my white poppy father
crying at your rage

And now at seventy
the Aldermaston Rd well trod

Your bed of white feathers
wet with tears
for so many treaties
and accords not met.

He knows peace who has forgotten desire.

Bhagavad Gita

Tribute To The Women Of Greenham

Nicola Daly

Night after Greenham night
In spite of our hunger, fear and fight
We sang through the frosty
Patchouli scented hours
For human rights.

Kosovo

Paul J King

(1) Exodus

A million workers rise
stand tall
      and leave

(2) Regeneration

Beside broken bridge
over which broken men have crossed
      a flower blooms

(3) The long march

A rainstorm sweeps down
canvas city
a thousand people
      globules of clay

(4) Canvas city

An autumn wind blows
and takes away
      the sounds similar

CNN

Emma-Jane Arkady

It's an escaped thing
an on ice eventing
absence of news,
is what happens – in your dreams now.
It's a version of vision
of lain in a bear strewn bed in the midst
of a tangled-rancid tossed-up failing day;
a vision of how it might scan,
it is a concept of escaping
over the hedge by next door's shed,
a dead fern on the florist's door, leaves
instead the salt-in-the-sugar mixture of bad
children, swilled
up in the cup of a stainless
metallic and bitter
taste to the edge to the teeth
of the world we inhabit
today,
listening to the news.

Kyrie Eleison

copland smith

I'm walking through Marie-Lou Park
kicking up leaves. Through the cool a poplar sways
while I hide in the yew-tree's dark.
I'm not watching the news today.

In each local shop, they say hello.
I meet friends along the way.
They say my name wherever I go.
I'm not watching the news today.

I'm out at Freshfield, walking the beach,
wrecking my shoes in Liverpool Bay,
striding into the sky. Out of reach.
I'm not watching the news today.

We lie together. It wasn't planned
and there are no words that I can say.
Lost on your eyes, lost to your hand.
No, I'm not watching the news today.

Three Portraits of Brian Keenan

Martyn Halsall

He is pictured below the poised arch of a rainbow,
Waits till it fades, dissolved by its own light.
You imagine all round him seven colours tinting
Details of fields, the evening coastlines.

Night falls. He has shepherded himself to a barn
And is looking back, to darkness, through the
      barred night.
Metal in the window frame becomes dark currency
He values as his memory weighs the cost of freedom.

He stands before us. Nervous. Quoting Beckett.
Opening the exhibition where the portraits speak.
He celebrates the photographer: 'It is almost as if
Like an Old Master he wills the light towards him.'

Outside, evening is drawn down, into the dock
Which turns to steel; a magnet gathering light.

Peace begins when the hungry are fed.

Anon

atrabilous

Philip Burton

when I see a skyscraper
burn like crepe paper
I'm atrabilous

and when Uncle Sam
kills a village Afghan
I'm atrabilous

-atrabilous?
        affected by bile
        Latin: bilus - bile
-'atrabilous'
        sounds like 'a-travel-risk'?
-atrabilous isn't this
it's 'being affected by bile'

see bile in the street?
you'd run a mile

I've had a bellyful
of atrabilous

tomorrow I'm going
to be affected
by caterpillars

instead

Menin Black

Philip Burton

He's felt the apologetic lurch
with which a plough
unearths a high explosive shell

but in a corner of a foreign field
that is forever dangerous
Luk shrugs, finishes the furrow.

He damps down the engine,
walks the long stir
of turned ground and bullish gulls.

He pauses, studies, frowns, turns
toward his rig,
at peace among the milling birds.

He pours coffee, unfolds breakfast
on a gingham towel.
Crisp dark bread. Sweet tomato

and today's gift from the hive.
His wide hands
cradle a muddied mobile phone.

He wipes it quiet, shields his eyes.
A NATO plane
glides between Armenti res

and the careless-lidded honey
of landscape
slowly finding its ancient level.

Walk On Grass

Seán Body

Noineens my father loved,
but secretly: the blunt-eyed daisies
too unsophisticated for serious

cultivation. He didn't think
them beautiful, but something
perhaps in their hardiness connected

with him. Something elemental
in their proliferation. Not heeding
the sign: *Keep Off The Grass.*

I've become observant of signs,
but today – perhaps it is the headiness
of light, the sudden summer – today,

quite deliberately and slowly
I walk on grass. The carefully-tended
well-kept-off bed of civic pride

yields to my presence, springs back.
I smell green – So at peace am I then,
so cleansed of the city, the half life,

the timidity, the ways marked out
for me. So filled with a simple joy
of being. I want to steal overnight

to places that daily wake to hatreds –
The Ormeau Road, The Falls, Garvaghey –
to quietly slip the notion

into sleeping heads, so morning
might rise to a gentle exorcism:
Please walk on the grass;

but first remove your shoes,
this ground is holy –
Tread lightly, touch the song.

Noineens: from *Nóinín* (Gaelic) A daisy

Too Young To Forget

Philip Burton

Come here, lad, I'm going to pin it on you.
Red for blood, black where the bullet's in.

Why would I want a bullet hole reminding
her of death? I hadn't had my living yet.
But I gave in. Rules of the asylum.
The flat waving fields wore them. So must I.

She showed me a sketch drawn
by Grandad, keeping his head low.
Distant windmill, two trees, a dusky river.
On white card then. Or yellow.

Tithed memories. All I had of him
has crumbled into beige chalk dust.
You see, I took the picture from its frame
as children do, as children must.

As war churned the landscape
he drew it back to life again. Somme Horizon.
Calm rye grass. No poppies. I walked
the long line, looking for him.

Give peace a chance.

John Lennon

Tropic

Susannah Marshall

In the frilly hotel room,
I covered your mouth
while our flesh kissed, wet
with sweat and sticky bliss.

Embarrassed by our noises –
raw, stripped calls,
I flicked on the TV;
a war film buzzed overhead.
With Spitfires and Hurricanes dog-fighting;
we loved with a lightness that was mocking.

Diesel filled our senses;
caked in sooted fug
the fondant hotel suite,
your buttered flesh
and scent of shortbread.

When the all-clear sounded,
we did not think of England,
with its stodge of history;
fields and front lawns;
maypoled traditions;
barley-seeded lores.
We washed-up in a place exotic;
tropic. Silent shores.

Last Night I Dreamed Violence Had Died

Willie A Rivers Jr

Is this reality, these things that I'm seeing,
Everyone here is actually treated like a human
    being.
No one's treated differently because of their
    complexion.
There are no more car alarms and no need for
    police protection.
Padlocks became outdated, there were no
    dictators to be hated.
People seemed astounded, just to be around what
    God had created.
Heroism replaced terrorism, there was no more
    guerrilla warfare.
No hunted foxes, or people in boxes, everyone
    lived somewhere.
No more anger or fear, they no longer existed.
The world was at peace because no one had
    resisted.
This new way of life, absent of struggle and strife.
No one's being strangled, or stabbed with a knife.
No more missing children, or women screaming
    RAPE!
No need for armed policemen, or crime scene
    yellow tape.
You could hear but a whisper, everything was so
    quiet.
No shooting or looting, in the aftermath of a riot.
There were peaceful demonstrations, no public

hangings or castrations.

No one bled or was left dead from any domestic
altercations.

There were no places that left any traces of
having a barbed wire fence.

No CCTV, how could this be, there was no need
for self-defence.

Conversation ruled every nation, never did they
collide.

No more Crown Courts, or any news reports of
multiple homicide.

No one contaminated the drinking water, no man
tried to molest his own daughter.

People didn't do things like robbing Burger
Kings, and no one committed manslaughter.

Was this only a vision, maybe a premonition, or
was I simply fantasising

Of a community, built on unity, without even
realising

That as I slept, those thoughts were kept inside
my conscious mind.

Not much time left, so I pinch myself, cause only
in a dream someone could find

A world that consisted of all the things I've listed,
peace and harmony existed world-wide.

Then my alarm went off, and I thought, don't be
soft,

Last night I dreamed violence had died.

He who knows no hatred needs no sword.

Gandhi

Moments: People

All works of love are works of peace.

Mother Theresa

Driving Through

Fran Pridham

As if forty years spent
watching a reflection slip away.
My hand reaches for that hand
that isn't mine
and shocks to feel the meat of me.

And driving home - the dark - the rain
I pass the Roxy cinema
the same, though smartened by time:
night driving always
takes me to my brother, Joe,
who loved to drive and chose a car
to kill himself.

I still haven't made the pieces fit
and sometimes choose to force them in
but as I turn the corner, pass
the flat I used to have,
something slips:

so this is peace:
the car, the road, the knowing;
always the slow drive home.

Grandma's Feet

Nii Parkes

On muslim knees
we knelt at her feet:
Sun-darkened, sand-hardened
and twitching in response
to fragrance bearing winds;
they told the tales
of a well trod earth.

The Line

Ra Page

10pm, dusk, the Wyke Regis
end of the Portland bridge. My brother is
crabbing; eyes down, his coat inflated
like a black sea slug before it's picked
up and squeezed. He sits, legs loose
and though he hears
he keeps the float in focus.

Sent to find him as the others shake sand
from their towels, I grab the rail, stand
up and lean out above him: the sea
just different histories turning up grey
mud. And out of it a single line
being fed slowly, dragged back in
by hand. The rest like moving stone,
like tarmac, fluid in the rain.

Peace is the only battle worth waging.

Albert Camus

The Beggar And The Ice-Cream Man

Tom Read

And though it was the end of the day
And though the ice-cream man was shutting the
      clacking shutters on his van
And though the ice-cream man wore a turban
      and the beggar wore a vest
And though the beggar liked ice-hockey, the ice-
      cream man loathed it
And though the ice-cream man's feet were size
      10, but the beggar's were only size 9
They managed to sit in the sunshine, enjoying an
      ice-cream together

The Last Time

Anjum Malik

Sitting beside my father, I watched his face
He asked me to shave his beard
Lathering his stubble, I moved slowly
savouring the shape of his jaw, his lips
his perfect mouth, as he lay there
we talked, reminiscing of the days when
I stood by him as a little girl
shaving my pretend beard
and we laughed remembering how I cried
when I realised I would never have a beard
to shave, of my own
I combed his hair, parting at the side
with my palms I patted on his aftershave
He sat up laughing
I lit a cigarette and placed it between his lips
he laid back and exhaled, smoke swirled slowly
Time was moving fast
there was almost none left
the last time I saw him
he was holding my mother's hands
they were smiling at each other.

Women Talking

Kay Bastin

Arm on the back of her chair
wrist strong relaxed
hand poised in air
lifts
gently
as they talk
comes to rest
softly
between her shoulders
connecting
absent-mindedly
caressing
returns
to lie on the back of her chair.

Peace cannot be kept by force. It can only be achieved by understanding.

Albert Einstein

At Night

Tariq Latif

Every now and again a knot cracks
And the burning sticks fall a little.
The old women and men go on talking
About who is to marry whom
And who has died and who has left...
Their tobacco rich voices mingle
With the world news on the radio.
The children, curled up by the fire,
Are lulled to sleep by the deep voices.

Around the farmers, in the immense dark,
There are the sleepy cotton fields;
Luminous cotton plants that look like stars
Afloat in the endless expanse of the Milky Way.
Fireflies wander among them like brief comets
Or souls dissolving just beyond ourselves.

Calm

Daisy Shortman

It was calm last night as we walked
home from church.
No more banging, whistling or
shouting as it normally had been
on a Tuesday night.

We thought it strange because it
had been like that for several months.

An enquiry should be made
because they could be lying there
gunned down by some evil one
whose heart is cold as the empty street.

So boldly I went about this enquiry
only to find two kittens in a wooden
box and a note which said
Be kind and feed them for us
we can't take any more.

One Of These Days

Helen Clare

It will be bright and cool. I'll wear cotton.
Fresh, as if miles were moments away.

You'll be in the garden, with muddied knees,
your face soiled where you paused to scratch your
        nose.

The washing will be out, I'll climb the steps
to the kitchen. The pots will be unwashed.

You won't have shopped. I'll put the kettle on,
find fruit and cheese at the back of the fridge.

Neither of us will say hello.

Night Music

Helen Clare

through a thin wall
I hear my parents snore

his chesty on the outstroke
silent on the inhale

hers lighter heady
whistles in purrs out

her rib cage rises
as his falls his breath

is released to the room
as hers is taken

only
his stroke is slower

than hers his rumble
lags until it rubs

against hers precedes it
like the double thump

and pause
of a heart beat

then in a moment
meets it

a single breeze
shifting the air

until with a shudder
the unease of bed springs

one kicks stretches
the other heaves their bulk

aside
and there's silence

before rumble
and purr resume

balanced   as before

And if they incline towards peace, incline thou also towards it.

The Holy Koran 8: 62

Last-But-One Patrol

David Bateman

There are rules against falling asleep
which to a nightwatchman seem fair
but as the black sky greys
above the opposite roofs
and I slump on elbows at the creaky old table
and as I move into my 35th hour awake
with the wetness of sleep pawing me
like the waves of an incoming tide,
I dream of my heaviness in dawn's sandy air
and of how light I would be
as each wave tugged me gently down the beach.
I'd float and bob in my heavy weightless clothes,
slip gently
beneath the squabble of air and water,
glide down and graze the burrows
of cockles, tube-worms, crabs;
sit in submerged dreams
at the same old creaky table I found there,
stand up again and walk weightlessly
through my last-but-one patrol,
a somnambulist security man
dutifully checking all the underwater windows,
returning as the tousled sky grows lighter
to the same old creaky table,
to sit there, gently sleeping
in saltwater rhythms and the dream
which is the dream of this poem
with its powers over the passage of time
and over sleeping and waking.

Overnight With You

Steve Anderson

I lie silently stroking your sleep
something makes you jolt -
I whisper and gentle your shoulder,
until peace reclaims you;
your breathing levels to a balance.

And when your silver car
has soared away into time,
I bury my face in still-damp towels,
smell again your body,
recall licking you in our shared shower.

Alone

Elaine Okoro

I breathe in the air consciously
and I am aware how it feels
        light and warm

As I lie on the bed...alone
I spread out and feel the space
I have to grow and stretch
So good I smile, is this what
loneliness means?

I hear every sound in the sound
I make
            To know every decision is mine
Is that what freedom is meant to be?
If I had dreamt it would be like this
I would have ended our time together, so much
        sooner then.

Do you want long life and happiness? Strive for peace with all your heart.

Psalm 34; 12,14

Star Matter

Tariq Latif

I lower her back slowly
Vertebra by vertebra. I unclamp
Her puffy legs and gently
Place her head on the damp
Stone ledge. I lift her arms
And cross her hands on her chest.
Her pale mouth, absent of the charms
Of love is puckered and messed.
Her eyelids are dark half moons; her skin
Folds and flows like a white desert. This could
Be the altar on which Abraham was to dim
The light from his son's life. I should
Be glad for not being the executioner and yet
This is worse, suffering the hot gasps
Of her wounded heart, wet
And trembling with no release to lapse
Into a painless sleep. I was going to tell
Her that these rocks are Mesozoic, elemental
Made from crushed stars which fell,
Cooled and gave life to life to skeletal
Life; that the hydrogen in water
Links us to the stars. But her breath remains
Faint, irregular and becomes shorter;
And even though below the earthy blood stains
On my palms there is the wisdom of my life,
It is of no use; useless; my idiot hands
Can do nothing to save my wife
Whose soul drips into the dark lands.

I place my mouth, onto hers, slowly
And let our breathing become one breath
From first to last, sacred and unholy
Hard and soluble, life and death
The same; as we were, as we are,
Weightless and heavy, bright and dark matter.

Dream Dream

David Bateman

Everything here happens twice:
once on the way there,
and once on the way back.
I'm dreaming that I've gone to sleep in the bath,
and that some other me is looking down
watching the ripples slowly spreading and
    returning to my gently snoring body.
In the other room, the radio is discussing
    stratagems for dealing with unemployment.
Being asleep, I am missing the programme
but do not mind, because I heard it yesterday.
I watch myself move slightly in my sleep.
Some slightly larger ripples move gently to and fro.
As far as I can make out,
I am in absolutely no danger of drowning.

Moments: Places

Go placidly amidst the noise and haste and remember what peace there may be in silence.

Desiderata

On Chorley Old Road

Rod Riesco

At a certain angle
of the evening sun
the carved red bricks
of Old Chorley Road
speak in the tongues of angels.

A boy on a scooter zips past.

Heading uphill, I remember
the dank aquarium
beneath the Central Library
where long grey fish
move smoothly
in green shop windows.

St Peter's Square

Louise V Mulvey

Last night the air was soft.
I stopped in the stillness,
Settled in the milky air.

In a square unpeeled of noise and people
buildings stood, steeped in the sunshine of the day,
solid in the empty evening.
Warm white pillars
held a moment
as whole as breath.

Llais Craig Yn Syrthiaw

copland smith

Half the slate in England, some time back,
was pulled by horses down a small canal
away from the sound of falling rock.

From this intruded granite hill
in a flashing silent film
I watch the black slope crack, begin its fall.

And I had hoped for breathless calm,
for peace to mourn the broken stone.
The rolling sound engulfs. Press nail to palm-

the roar subsides. The moan
turns heads in a further valley.
they falter, silenced one by one-

each man who hears his father calling.
Llais craig yn syrthiaw-
the voice of the rock in falling.

When the power of love overcomes the love of power the world will know peace.

Jimi Hendrix

hillside transformation

John Siddique

our heavy feet
stumble, startling deer
climbing the hill
we struggle with, with light leaps
perfect muscular explosions

their brown merging with the fern
they stop to watch us through shrub
their stillness creates rock

we watch each other
each with the right to be
in this becomes a prayer

we know each other
on these skylines
each other's fear on display
my head turns with antlers and
muscular neck to face my companion
deer's face to man's face
with the turn of a head

At Etherow

Steve Waling

The place I'm thinking of
- you know it too - a park with ducks
and a lake that stretches into canal,
mill-race, odd signs of industry,
where I always walk to the top. One
rare day of sun, I found myself
wandering, and discovered -
through greeny tunnels of willow -
another lake - so still

it was almost nowhere
except for swans who claimed it
as a nest. I want to bring you here
but I'd intrude on
someone else's calm,
I ought to go. No sound
except white bodies slipping into lake,
or birds I can't identify.

I want to bring it to you: this feeling,
maybe it's closer than we think:
just under or beyond, or around the next...

Sirius

Jan Whalen

Hurrying past the back alleys
to avoid the Levenshulme drunks
I spotted a silent herd of wheelie bins
huddled in a midnight gathering.
Meanwhile the dog star
low and brilliant overhead
following Orion, faithful as ever
will still be there tomorrow.
Strangely, this is enough.
Any small bit of continuity:
however brilliant,
however tin foil
the constellations.

Whalley Abbey

Helen Clare

We pass through a place
where a gate might have hung,
and on to consecrated ground.
We tread lightly
on the grass-healed footsteps
of the past. The felled walls
are low as paths, smooth,
it is hard to know
whether we walk within rooms
or between rooms. Heartsease,
ivy grow on tumbled stone.
Sometimes a corbel shows
the position of a floor, blackening
suggests fire. It seems
there are traces of prayer.

By the chapter house,
a boy flies a huge kite. It tugs
on its string, rolls and rises,
marks in magenta
the unseen currents in the air.

Helsinki

Sue Ann Harding

the bay is white
the sunken horizon dipping away
from the cathedral dome
from wefted clouds blown
not blue, not light blue
over the widening band of the ice harbour
where ships rock, locked.

and here now, and here
behind a window glass
the dayboat docks
at the ruins of our lovers' bed
your breath beside me, and we
washed between latitudes of hope

are a double droplet of rain
cleft tenderly apart
rift in the pale light.

The coastal, strata waters back
the forward lap.

When you clench your fist, no one can put anything in your hand.

Alex Haley

Unexpected

Lynne Taylor

The house tenses, listens to a softer step,
witnesses an unfamiliar silhouette
fumbling. Click. Gloom, shocked into light,
glares at this intrusion.

Slowly, she lowers her bag. Does not want
to further disturb unsettled serenity.

A mug, half full of coffee, gapes
in undisguised coldness. A jacket hangs
in memory of a shape. Not hers.

Jagged silence clamours to be calmed.

She sifts CDs in a rumpled pile
chooses, stops, puts back. Presses 'play'
to hear what had last been heard.

Pure green notes. The 23rd psalm.
She crumples, covers her face, sobs.

The house is eased. Appeased, settles.
She wipes her eyes, switches on his kettle.

Trying The Couch

Ra Page

The video display guides me safe
through a new dark. One blanket's enough;

a cushion between the knees. Instead of trying
to be elsewhere, back in bed, I'm going

to just sit here, with a beanbag
so large to stare at. A live multiplug

signals its position under the TV.
Long curtains hang on a day

that hasn't spoken yet, as I invite
my arm to drop slowly, trawl the carpet.

Elsewhere, in the lava lamp, perfect
silhouettes prolong themselves in tact,

like this dead couch and the bean bag that sits
indented by the curve of dull thoughts.

The coffee table stands still as it should,
its cloth reaching lower on one side.

Marazion

Colin Jones

Mortar which lasts, holding together ancient stone,
which might have known the blast before the
      treasure,

lichen rings growing in shades of green.

Listen, go and do not trouble,
your life the smallest circle there.

Nothing

Charles Bennett

I'm watching a wren
flicker around the branches
of the crab apple tree
in our back garden.

Next door but one
spent most of the morning
ticking off his roses
with a pair of secateurs.

At the end of his garden
a bonfire smoulders
from the bottom of a galvanised dustbin.
Nothing is happening

just at the moment
which is fine by me –
the blossom will come
when it's ready,

sooner or later
the fruit will be home.
The smoke has its own sour music
to which a ginger cat

is listening. Meanwhile
the wren goes flittering
round each of the naked branches
in no particular order.

For Monika

Bettina Jones

Great-grandma's bungalow
had dark and glowing rooms
gaslight and flickering flames
treasure-trove mantelshelves
and always the scent of roses.

My nana's bay-windowed house
gleamed sunshine-yellow candlewick
polished leather chairs
let in clean sharp air
and the scent of roses.

My mother's home with a through lounge
was bursts of sunburnt orange
bright scatter cushions
psychedelic paintings
but still carried the scent of roses.

And I am housed in all of these
wrapped around enfolded safe
with something of myself to give
to my daughters when they come -
I am the smallest Russian doll to date
rooted deep in roses.

Friendship improves happiness and abates misery, by the doubling of our joy and the dividing of our grief.

Cicero

An Irish Breakfast

Liz Loxley

Awake...but teetering on the edge of sleep–
Like an island teased by two climates:
The westerly winds of the Atlantic;
The warming currents of the Gulf Stream.

Your palms bring sunshine to my skin.
Your fingers trip along the keys of my spine,
Tip me into wakefulness, spill me into the day
Like an egg cracked into a china mug.

We breakfast in the snug.
The froth of the Guinness laps at our lips
         like the tip of a wave.
The salt mucus of oysters, slippery as seaweed,
Trickles down our throats,
Dribbles,
Slithers.

Bath

Rosie Lugosi

White as the inside of a cup; one from
the back of the cupboard. I lean over, my hand
on the cigarette burns beading the lip.
Squeeze in the black frayed plug. Steam clouds
the tiles I grouted to save money. Thundering

water covers up the scratches from where
I dropped the hammer, and the ceiling plaster
stamped in by cowboy builders all the Ajax
of Arabia will not shift. I drip in
five drops of lavender. The label says

relaxing. Perch on the edge and wait;
throat bitter from the oil. At seven inches
deep the tank is empty. The red tap
dribbles like an old man. The water heavy
against my palm as I swirl, calculating

how much cold I can get away with.
I step in with gritty feet; think, *must vacuum
that mat.* Lie with my knees bent; sit
with legs stretched out. I can't have both.
As I grow tepid, liquid collects on the wall.

The Japanese Garden

Muhammad Khalil

We arrived at the Japanese garden via an old
      English garden...

it was the only way in/ that is/ there was no other
      way from the
direction we had come/ in fact from any direction...

so we lingered and spent some time there first.

We sat on a roughly hewn wooden bench/ in a
      walled garden/ red brick/
pleasantly evocative...

childhood memories/ Sunday school/ Sunday
      afternoons/ Sunday roast/ C.S.
Lewis and after tea Dickensian serials on the tv.

We sat and we talked/ travelling back through
      the pastiche wardrobe of
our post-colonial minds to a pre-Narnian time of
      Lions/ gas-lamps and
snow chimes....... then through into the Japanese
      Garden.

It was a good experience. The contrast was
      pleasing in itself/ the
difference/ well that was an education.

I had always admired the Japanese sense of

minimal maintenance...
The impression of random order...
the intuitive sense of composition...
that arose
from the Zen philosophy.

The creation of a microcosm/ or mini-landscape/
        based on an observation
of the ordering strategies of nature itself.

Nature.../ The contrived accident.

I remember somebody telling me that/ 'all good
        ideas are arrived at by
accident.'
The Japanese seemed to take this as a rule of thumb.
Serendipity.
Something/ I felt/ they seemed to have in
        common with the great 'Jazz'
maestros of the past.

As synchronicity would have it/ only that very
        week I had composed my
very first successful haiku...
after several weak attempts.

This seemed like a perfect place to perform it.
The whole occasion had a sense of ritual about it.
Maybe it was the internal events of the bus
        journey/ who knows.

All I knew was that today I felt like there was
beauty in everything...

and life was
precious, ever so
precious. Like a
precious stone hard but beautiful to behold

Humour

My therapist told me a way to achive inner peace was to finish things I had started. Today I finished a sponge cake, a bottle of Vodka and a box of Milk Tray.

Anon

The Right Thing

David Bateman

She says she knows it's late
but she's phoning me to get
my friend's number.
She has some information for him,
information that won't wait.
He is a bastard
and he needs to be told,
needs to be told right now.
I decide not to go into
how all of our needs are
relative to our goals
or even into just how keen
she was to be introduced
a mere four hours ago
but I do probably pull a face at this point.
It's 3.30 a.m.
and while I'm trying to talk her out of it
it occurs to me that here is a woman
who is not only spurned
but also pissed as a fart
which is a bad combination fury-wise,
and may well put Hell
out of the running altogether.
Certainly she won't take No
and certainly I do pull a face now
even if I didn't before.
It is necessary to cave in,
but fortunately I have drunk

nearly as much as she has
and now the alcohol comes to my aid,
as suddenly I know exactly what to do,
and saying Just a moment,
I haul out the Yellow Pages
flop it open at random,
and read off the first local number.
As we say Goodbye I study
the simple line drawings
of conservatories and patio doors.
She will not get
my friend just yet but she will
get double glazing if she likes.
Tomorrow she will thank me for this
and as I put down the phone
it occurs that neither anger
nor double glazing could ever equal
that warm feeling you get inside
from knowing
you've done the right thing.

Recollections In Tranquillity

David Bateman

Now some poets type, but instead,
I do *my* writing all in my head,
    Thus I can compose
    All my poems and prose
Without once getting up out of bed.

The price of peace is the cost of a pair of earplugs.

Anon

Blue Grass Blues

Philip Burton

I'd live in grass that's thistle-blue,
heave buckets to flush the john
watch the wide Missouri
as it ambles broadly on.

I hunger for hootenanny
where night is hot and long
and belt-and-braces canny
men to tell me when I'm wrong.

I hanker for candy-crunch washboards,
and banjos like peppery spoons.
I yearn to roll on cobs of corn
with cousins in tumble-down barns.

I yearn for young Virginia
with a rip in her cargo jeans
a hickory lap-top processor
and her rocking chair that leans.

I'd live in grass that's thistle-blue,
heave buckets to flush the john
watch the wide Missouri
as it ambles broadly on.

The Coconut's Dream...

Philip Burton

for peace

I, the dark moon of coral-fringed bays
wish to tie my hair in sand
and whistle the wind through my palm
before they have my fibre flat under their feet
my flesh in their mouths, my milk poured
from mouth to nipple. My route is clear.
My plan is a mad hope for the dead.
The sea is always in the dusty market corner
of my swollen eye, pressing its till-drawer
on the stall-keeper's paunch.
He grinds his gouty toes with salt
curling the stripes of caftan for a comb.
His beard is white as womb's milk is white
white as the grazing sea. His fingers chase a
      spinning coin
that glides in prayer, a silver nun. Oh, pray for me.
But his hand comes down like a monkey's rotten
      stick
ringing the bell of a dying horse-fly.
When will the shy monsoon gale come by
and bowl me down the penny-pinching hill
into the rough sea's eye? I'd whirl out on the
      tidal mounds.
I'd go where dolphins go, free from the drift-net's pull.
A brooch on the swirling Cape. Calm as you will.
Going as the dark moon to coral-fringed bays
to tie my hair in sand and whistle the wind
      through my palm.

Approaching Haiku

Peace comes from within. Do not seek it without.

Buddha

two drifting snowflakes

Lynne Taylor

two drifting snowflakes
meet by chance in a slow fall
on a white blanket

Moments

Melanie Duncan

Your index finger
As it strokes the side of my face
Followed by a butterfly kiss

Day dreaming about you,
The darkness of your skin
Smooth to the touch

The warm scent of you
I call up
When I need to remember

Chernaya Rechka
(Black River)

Sue Ann Harding

bare feet walk across
    a wooden floor

unlit candles
    wait for fire

balcony beckons
    every earlier dawn

there is such hope
    in the space between rooms

passing time

Shamshad Khan

my mother at the table
my father at the table
legs crossed
shelling peas

A Father's Peace

SuAndi

Cradled
Wrapped in arms of pure pride
Textured layers of all I got is yours
Coming daily
Flowing out
Charged by your waking cry
Burped surprise after food is done
For the moment
Each moment
Is precious in your presence
For before this
Life had love
Now love is everlasting

Chill

Chanje Kunda

Hot bath
Spliff
Post orgasmic
Bliss

Hot bath
Bliss
Post orgasmic
Spliff

Glimpses of Peace

Roy Howard

Heaviness dulls me
till I follow my breathing
and let peace break in.

Insomniac, I
burn incense and read
dark night becomes dawn.

At the Arndale Centre:
your books are boring!
give me shops, bright lights,
tea, fags: paradise.

Peace heals, elevates, and invigorates the spirit.

Michael DeBakey

abandon thought

Shamshad Khan

watch clouds drift

    know what drifting is

That Moment Of Peace

Lucy Koniarska

Gleaming
in the caress of
sunlight coming through the kitchen window
three newly washed rice bowls
coiled around each other
just waiting to dry.

A Good Night's Sleep

Ian McDonald

Everybody's clock's set differently
In this 24 hour society.

You've no right to a night's sleep:
It has to be negotiated.

Tomorrow, a landlord to see about the thickness of
insulation between me and 'him' upstairs.

Mythical-Mystical-Chemical

The Great Way has no gate. Clear water has no taste. The tongue has no bone. In complete stillness, a stone girl is dancing.

Seung Sahn

The Return Of The Doves

John Lyons

1

She knew always
that he would come, her non-identical twin.

When he did, he was like a hurricane,
havoc and pillage on his mind.
Doves rose in a flutter of feathers, whitewashed
the sky dark-greying with smoke.

She was squatting under a tamarind tree
weaving coconut mats.
She offered no resistance.
He dragged her across wounded fields,
pulping under-foot the flesh of yams.

'Your healing, nurturing ways
disgust me,' he snarled.

11

Long ago, armed with pen and metaphor,
Aristophanes wrote a play:
He sent Trygaeus, the farmer,
on a giant dung beatle in search of Peace.
She was found in an abandoned pit roofed with stones.

Amidst the feasting,
one by one the doves returned.

The Oldest Women Of The World

Liz Almond

Seer, not seen, transitional;
not yet one of them.
OK. I'll put on a dress with sleeves
and a dipped hem, but please may mine be silk?
Cotton's too dull, too opaque–
from the bodies of worms
I acquire my sheen; lustrous,
the cloth ripples across my thigh
hiding bulbous vein and marbled
fat that has a name
redolent of praying orders.
Old Cassandras, we cocoon our own flesh.

Take a sandal. A youthful shoe,
all straps and tiny buckles,
keeper of the varnished toe nail,
concealer of horn. Callous.
Take a chopstick in a twist of hair.
The point of view is aeriel,
an opening shot from mountain peak
makes her determined
as long as her boots last,
and her feet go one before the other.

Blood on the pillow reminds me
of the daughter's dilemma:
season of eggs pulsing
out from their follicles.
I have gone beyond egg and blood
into a time of stretched linen.

Lucy Locket

Jean Rees

Every girl of nine earth-cycles, without
a room of her own, is entitled to pockets.

In my red and green waistcoat, with matching
waspie belt, I kept notebooks with pressed
      clover
between the leaves, photographs of friends,
and letters *sealed-with-a-loving-kiss* from
      Victor.

One September day in my garden, by father's
begonia metallica, everything changed.
A boy from the alley rifled my secrets.

I emptied my precious pockets, tore each letter
into fragments which I let fly like a thousand
pieces of shrapnel across the backs of Addison
      Crescent.

Lately, I see the crescent on the flag of Islam,
and watch children, nightly, quartering the sand
for the ring pull of the spent bomb-de-terre.

These days, I never un-pick the pockets on my
      new Versace,
tailored to fit like the flak jacket into which they

stitch a
lining, worn next to the thigh, for walking the
        killing fields

where armoured cars without shutters spit at the
        blackened
windows of Shuhada Street, Hebron, make
        widows for
Tunnel Road, Jo'burg. And there is no armistice
        for Armagh.

Hear no evil, see no evil, says Saint Lucy of Syracuse.

So, carry palms to the Cave of Patriarchs, gossip
    in the Kasbah,
make peace with the oppressor behind enemy
    lines; paint your lips
of steel with velvet, wear a purple battle-dress
    and helmet, and dance

in your burqua, your saree, your shift; move
    through the savannah,
the ghetto, ground zero, wearing silent shoes,
    safe in the knowledge
that your bio-purse nurses an embryo of dreams.

Breathing Space

Ra Page

Like when you set a camera up,
bring an eye to the view-finder
but seeing nothing, half-wonder
if the world beyond the lens-cap

(still on) is there... Or maybe I mean
the gap you speak into sometimes
between far-off rings when it seems
they've picked up, then it rings again;

or flicking channels, that black-screen
background just as the last ad
gives way to the Welcome Back; that bide
for playing time before Track 1

(*is it on pause?*); or when you can't
tell if the other's under a bridge
or merely taking time to gauge
their answer. I mean before the count

of Big Ben, of those seven bleeps,
when you've tuned in just to hear
the headlines (three seconds to spare)
and miss the link, the traffic tips,

and catch what can only be the hiss
of shuffled papers, the airwaves breathing:
it's like there's someone there, soothing
you by staying close. There is.

We have drunk soma and become immortal;
we have attained the light, the Gods discovered.

Rig Veda

Chlorpromazine

Emma-Jane Arkady

Carefully dosed-out
a precise count-out I find with its effect
a lasting five hours of bliss, followed
by the quick dip in a pool of
Christ-its-cold anxiety.

Its got a bad name, this lightening
with its lifting of the sharp-dark sprung
from the broken tree as a jagged
branch, it is a soother at these small titrations
[my psychiatrist's word which I think
means measure], is as I said,
a bliss.

But then and according to holy word
I have to wait for a shite single hour
for the next, all, guessing the state of the world
logging on to the breaking-news, fretting-sick
feared-up, pacing, ripping at the spitting page
from the laser with a fucking paper, jam;
a vicious worry-ball of knot in the heart.

And then the clock says now and I take
out their little golden case [I bought them
this for their holy effect deserved a tabernacle]
place, the taste of soon-to-be-clean, pill
on my desk, take by mouth the salving, drift
off as the minutes tick quite slowly, to the reverie
the distancing of Cruise dreams, the fret gone, drift.

As I said, it has a bad name, they used to call it
The Chemical Cosh, which is true, when slammed
in as into a cell [see my earlier poem
Four Weeks of Mania stanza 1], is as abusive, but not
when gifted gentle like this; my precious white I
        write on –
just like now!

Counting On Peace

Liz Loxley

2 fingered peace sign
2 taps running into a lavender scented bath
2 swans necking
2 people hugging in snow
3 coins in a fountain on a Roman holiday
3 Wisemen having followed their star
4 limbs in perfect alignment
4 horsemen of the Apocalypse dismounting
6 bullets removed from a pistol
9 x 11 red balloons
13 unlucky for none
21st century unfurling like a baby's fist

Avatars

Pete Kalu

easing on my late grandfather's shirt
back seat of the midnight 83
power failure at Riley's 8 Ball Pool Palace
the last but one cigarette
No. 60 of 60 monthly payments
Round 10, 2 mins, 59

Junction 8 of the M66, 5am, light crosswind
Joshua, 57 days, belly full and burped
Fat licks of July rain

Milton Ubanatu contemplating his 486 screensaver
Small grey mouse in small black mouse trap

the last shared sputnik spliff before we hike

Me And The Meds

Ian McDonald

It's a kind of magic, when I've missed my meds.
I walk with a spring in my step.
Everything's beautiful.
Colours are richer.
Music is more intense.
But the downside is the fear.
Or being hypersensitive to what people say.
My mood can flick one way or the other.
But at least I feel alive sometimes.

Oscillating from one extreme to another.
I'm never able to stay at Nirvana for too long.
When I reach this place, my 'self' is dissolving.
My borders are weak, so I best not hang around
        here for too long.
It's time to go back up the scale in the opposite
        direction.
Me and my meds: can't live with it, can't live
        without it.

Peace is not only better than war, but infinitely more arduous.

George Bernard Shaw

The Pieces In-Between

Dike Omeje

The knowledge between the question and the answer
The rhythm between the music and the dancer
The distance between 2 fighters b4 they close it
The thought the writer conjured but never wrote it

The eye contact between the sniper and his target
The common ground between the fiction and the fact
The sound b4 the stock exchange opens the market
The clarity b4 addiction takes you back

The moment just b4 2 lovers say those 3 words
The spaces in-between performance and applause
When the cup that I thought was half empty *still*
    quenches my thirst
The knowing smiles on faces I thought my words
    had lost

The lessons I learn between instinct and instruction
The path between the professional and the beginner
The virgin's final stop b4 corruption
The road between the good man and the sinner

When I accept that the shoe fits, then wear it proudly
When I'm graceful in my rise *and* in my fall
The deadly sin that searched but never found me
The deadly sin that rose each time *I* chose 2 call

The gaps that fill the spaces between emotions
The wake that frees the reality of the dream
The magic that *still* works without the potion
The peace is in the pieces in-between.

The Narrow Road

Rosanna Imogen Wright

There walked two men upon a road,
The road too narrow for both their load,
So one man stepped to the nearest side.

Now with space, the man moved on,
And shot a glance to the other man,
'Peace my brother,' are the words he spoke,
'What trouble this narrow road could provoke.'

Sandalwood

Pete Kalu

Just strap hanging on a train
Nothing on my mind, nothing in the frame

Then She

Thru a cloud of blue smoke
Twisted tips of a bushy Afro
Then two natural lips, a mohair top
A body moving in fine flow

In front of me
I drew a breath

Brother, she said, u look tense,
U need to find some peace in your life
U need to open yourself to peace, let go of all
your strife

Peace? Sister, I'm a trainee software engineer
If I can't put a number on it, I don't want to hear

She said, come closer, and she placed an arm
around my waist
Relax your shoulders, she said, let your eyelids
fall, breathe without haste

Eyes closing, I felt - I felt a pressure on my lips,
warm, cushioning, bold

And every knot in every muscle began to uncurl,
        to unfold.

There, she said, that moment you experienced is
        peace
Now you know it, you will thirst for it again
And Brother, its number is the number of petals
        on all the lotus buds
The number of lovers on all the park benches
        across the world
Its number is infinite, a number you will aspire to
        attain

And I thought, Mmm - if that is peace, I'm a
        follower, I'm a convert
And I wanted to express this feeling to her that,
        on this, we were totally one
But my lips were so numb from her kiss
I couldn't talk - and in that moment she was gone

And I vowed to myself, from now and for the rest
        of my life
Looking for her, looking for peace, will be my
        only goal
And I will search the Earth with all my heart
And all my spirit and with all my soul

I'm still searching.

Hide your body in the Big Dipper.

Zen saying

The Poets About Their Poems

Liz Almond

Poetry is wrested out of me: the process is a gradual movement through rough notes and germs of ideas towards a meaning. I don't know where that movement will come to rest, but I know I am often looking for ambivalence. The poem here derives from a dream and explores ageing and how to be at peace with yourself.

Steve Anderson

All my poetry reflects raw honesty about my life. When I write it releases something very special hidden deep inside me. The fewer re-writes I do the cleaner and more pure the poem. I strive to clearly show readers the fuller picture so my biggest problem is editing.

SuAndi

My poetry is as impetuous as my personality. Some days it flows like rain in Manchester other days it's as stubborn as sunshine (again in Manchester), a half forgotten memory. I am a watcher of people. As with the doting father of Ylan Zayd Isaac (Little Billy{USA}) and thought, 'ah if only we all had such power of love'.

Emma-Jane Arkady

I write poetry because I love being published, it's great for my self-esteem, really gives me a buzz, especially my full-length collection from *Arc*. Writing seems to be an easy thing though it's based on a foundation of reading. I can write at will though sometimes have long spells when I can't be bothered at all. A dedication? For libraries everywhere, I'd be nowhere without them.

Kay Bastin
My poems usually come as an outburst in the heat of intense feelings, or as a reaction to an event. Sometimes they sneak up on me, like this one. I was sat behind these women and was mesmerised by the connection and tranquillity between them. Here's to peace in all its forms!

David Bateman
I worked three months as a nightwatchman in a big old terraced house in Huskisson Street in Liverpool 8. As a writer, it was a very productive time for me. *Last-But-One Patrol* is one of the few pieces I wrote about the job itself. I was incredibly tired, and the act of writing the poem was the main thing keeping me awake.

Charles Bennett
I try to hear the particular music of each poem. I try to rise early and go to my desk before work. The poem in this book is what happens when you look out of the window. Even now, somewhere near you, nothing is happening. Which is fine by me.

Seán Body
In an earlier poem I wrote '...as if we bear a disabling load. // Memory / nursed like a need...' More accurately, *history,* which is packaged

memory. *Walk on Grass* is deliberately naïve and simple minded. Cleansed of all impositions of history, culture and social conditioning, it simply embraces living. It is a prayer.

Cathy Bolton
Sometimes poems just happen to me in the back of cabs, but usually I have to tease them out through writing exercises. Writing to a set of instructions can feel very forced but it just takes one line or image to take root and the words become organic.

Philip Burton
i like a poem to scuff my shoes, drag me across lunar surfaces, pistol-whip my senses, stand me on my head in an alley, or am i thinking of movies?

Helen Clare
I write poetry to honour what is within me and to connect with what is around me. It's a place to indulge a little madness and a why to stay sane. I like poetry that touches or challenges me, that shifts or expands my perception of the world, but - crucially - allows me to think for myself. I suspect that poetry is a strange obsession, but it works for me!

Nicola Daly
I find writing poetry an exhilirating yet magical experience. I write poetry in the hope of igniting sparks in the hearts and minds of others. Poems such as this one are born from passion rather than experience. This poem is dedicated to the brave women of Greenham.

Philip Davenport

Accidental poems - ad slogans, misspellings, conversations - surround us. I just note them down. This poem is made from newspaper stories about September 11th.

Melanie Duncan

"You have always had the ability to write expressing such feeling....." "You can't not write ...it's in your blood, it would be such a waste if you didn't." These comments were made by people who knew me during my formative years and have encouraged me to share through poetry and prose. Writing has become my vehicle to articulate what I think, in the hope that I can inspire in the way that I have been inspired.

Poppy Fitzpatrick

Make Love Not War was written on an old paper bag - quickly scribbled down and later very slightly tidied up. I felt so strongly about the subject that the words formed themselves clothing the poem. To truly love is the greatest defence of all but the hardest to achieve.

Martyn Halsall

Both as a poet and a journalist I try to tell stories which raise issues, and provoke people to respond to them. Most of my poems begin with an incident, which reflects ideas. Good poetry intrigues, by taking a fresh look at our world and posing supplementary questions.

Sue Ann Harding
My ideas come from fleeting images - the memory of an apartment, a city, a beach - but the poems are only created through work and attention. I choose and delete words until the image or mood is clear on the page, a bit like looking through a camera lens: focusing and unfocusing and finally focusing.

Roy Howard
Poetry for me flows around your body, seeps from your fingers to your pen. It should come from the heart in no premeditated way. If it is good it talks. I paint, write and play music the same way, I hope others hear.

Bettina Jones
I think of myself as a wordsmith - a trade to be proud of - and my passion is poetry. I love exploring the word, the image, the line and the final shape; the sharing and workshopping and sending the poem out into the world to fend for itself.

Colin Jones
Poetry is a means of expressing both meaning and unmeaning, it answers the questions that fall between the two, and should side with neither but fly with each, for everyone's sake. I would like my poems to perform this function.

Pete Kalu
I had some rodent running around under my bedroom carpet at night and no light bulbs. It had me scared. I took up a hammer meaning to whack

it dead. But every time I got close, the rodent ghosted off. Finally I caught it full on with the blunt end, and took up the carpet. It was a tiny mouse. I felt so guilty. My poems are the mouse.

Graeme Kenna

Most of my poems hark back to my roots as a comedy writer; they're based around a punchline, and no, they're still not funny. *When Will There be Peace* is far from typical of my writing; but it was written on 11/9/01, which was a far from typical day.

Muhammad Khalil

What does poetry mean to me ? It means a healing path to self knowledge. It means the spontaneity of the African way of orality that gave birth to Jazz. It's a form of devotional activity, and a form of occupational therapy. My poetry helps heal the emotional wounds, and mental scar tissue of years of cultural misrepresentation, racist abuse, and abberant decoding. As such my most common inspiration for writing, is as a basic act of 'survival'. It's my instinctive way of mapping the 'self'. Keeping my sense of who I am, as a Blackman, and as a Muslim, in an oppressively soul destroying, culturally dry environment. This is who I am, what I'm about.

Shamshad Khan

The poems I write are either very very short or long. In consideration of the trees around the world the shorter ones are used in anthologies. The longer poems are for performance where the words are spoken out loud and the carbon dioxide produced is then available for the trees that haven't been cut down.

Paul J King
Wherever there is light, there is shadow; wherever there is length, there is shortness; wherever there is conflict, there is...? Bloodstains cannot be removed by more blood; resentment cannot be removed by more resentment. *Kosovo* is just a snapshot; I hope the images are different for everyone who reads it.

Lucy Koniarska
Although I have written poetry since childhood I have produced very few poems. I read and listen to other people's poetry much more than I write. I love the way poems can capture, and then share, something - some truth, some beauty, or some humour. *That Moment of Peace* is dedicated to Benjamin Zephaniah.

Chanje Kunda
Born in Zambia, I came to the UK when I was 5 years old. I try to paint the world in words with vibrancy and a funky imagination from an afro-centric female perspective. My poems are jazzy reflections on modern day living.

Tariq Latif
Writing poetry is safer than jumping out of a plane (with a parachute!) but the buzz you get when you

get it right on the page and in performance is something else. I love it...and like love poetry is illusive and found nowhere and everywhere! Enjoy!

Liz Loxley
I enjoy writing/reading poetry for the sense I can make of this confusing world. I like connections, similes, metaphors, images. For example, a partly eaten slice of melon reminds me of someone's spine, a viaduct of someone's teeth. A quick thanks to my mum for the poetry writing genes.

Rosie Lugosi
I find poetry harder to write than fiction, but then some days I find the effort of shopping lists make my teeth clench. When I write, I do a rough version, forget all about it, then rediscover it months later and rewrite completely. I think of it as a composting-down time. Yes, I like gardening too.

John Lyons
The inspiration for a poem is only the beginning. After that is the fine art of word-crafting. It is a process which I thoroughly enjoy. The poem becomes a distillation of words, feelings and ideas, like good strong bush rum, and a heady pleasure to read.

Ian McDonald
Poetry is like having an epileptic attack. It's very private and can anybody really fathom what the hell you're talking about?

Anjum Malik

Mostly I don't go about writing poetry, poems just arrive. Sometimes they wait a long time for me to have the courage to let them through, like the one about my father, which took over twenty years. I have never written poems with any intentions of what they might do, but I do love it when I read them out and the listeners connect, react. It's a fantastic feeling to touch others with your own words. The poem is dedicated to my father.

Susannah Marshall

I started off writing poems in felt-pen when I was four, about monsters and ghosts and witches. These days my subject matter and writing implement has changed. I usually get the first line of a poem in my head and leave it fermenting in there, not really thinking about it until at some point it reminds me it's around and then I put pen to paper and a poem appears. I never really know what they're going to be about until I have a page full of words. Usually, they finish up being about love. Dedicate *Tropic* to all those I love, particularly the guy who invented chocolate.

Louise V Mulvey

It starts with noticing. Walking, on a train or at a tram stop, I see something and I write it down. Then I drift off to the feeling or thought it evokes; that's how poems start. This particular evening was so still and so rare that it made me stop.

Elaine Okoro

Poetry starts as a tapping in my head and before I can do anything (God forbid this is anything to do with me being a woman) I have to tidy-up. So I've cleared a space for my mind - very important. The connection with myself and other people begins, from pen to paper.

Dike Omeje

Words make me powerful like Samson or beautifully cunning like Delilah. May take you centuries 2 fathom but just a moment 2 decipher. Similes and metaphors fight 4 the cause or cause the fighting. I feel like keys that open doors or knives that open wounds when I am writing.

Ra Page

For me the challenge, when writing verse, is to try and make things as pedestrian as possible without losing the poetry. The natural, and lazy, urge when trying to write is always towards the overly metaphoric and the over-adventurous, which makes for bad writing in my case. Besides, the most mundane things are also the most potent when you re-approach them. *The Line* is dedicated to Lytton, the ever-fisher, *Trying the Couch* to my girlfriend's love of 70s decor.

Elizabeth Parish

Words are important to me. I write because it seems necessary to do so, and because it helps me to understand what I really think and feel. I like the compactness of good poetry. I try to write regularly, sometimes using recognised poetic forms in the hope that this will give my ideas shape, and sometimes letting my mind wander.

Nii Parkes
Shaded from the Ghanaian sun by neem trees, I honed my talent for poetry writing love letters for uncouth boys keen to win the hearts of well- spoken girls.

Fran Pridham
My idea of poetry? Well, life strings moments together like a collection of beads and poets it seems can't resist writing about them! Why? Martin Stannard puts it well. For him writing is, 'not letting a good part of me rust away,' and I feel that too!

Tom Read
A simple poem. Too simple maybe? Maybe that's the point. You can't solve all the world's problems with ice-cream, but it might help. Written following a real event, the image struck a resonant chord (I guessed the feet sizes).

Jean Rees
Poetry, for me, is the theatre of words: conveying a drama in miniature to be enjoyed for its imagery and surprise, or squirrelled away for later pleasure long after the book is closed. I love the 'experience' of poetry, and I hope that my work expresses secret places, as well as the stories of life.

Rod Riesco

What is the real world that is, and isn't, the world we see? Call it 'peace' if you like. Sometimes I see a glimpse of it and try to write it. With luck and work, you catch a glimpse of a glimpse. Ah! Peace at last, till the next time.

Willie A Rivers Jr

Daisy Shortman

In the poem featured in this collection I was walking down a noisy street that was usually quiet. My imagination took over as I specualated on the cause of the disturbance.

John Siddique

I was born of Indian and Irish heritage in the latter half of the twentieth century in a small northern backwater. I appreciate extremes: dub, buffy the vampire slayer, people with opinions, Japanese noise music, olives, halloumi cheese and ripe avocados. I like people and words that reveal truth, even fictitious truth, that tell me something new about something that's become the same old song.

Lemn Sissay

I sometimes get asked. What's my favourite poem. This is my answer. My favourite poem is the one I am working on. And the last one I wrote is the one I always wanted to write. I hope and pray that I will never write my favourite poem.

copland smith

Peace, man. Hard topic. Liked the challenge of it. I usually use form and rhyme to tie up my conscious, and see what the unconscious feeds into the structure. Me: born 1953 Liverpool, lived everywhere including Nigeria, won a few competitions, writing crime now. And death-poems. I like death.

Lynne Taylor

I love to read a poem and think *Yes!* and admire how exquisitely that empathetic feeling has been induced. In writing poetry I try to plumb a connection between inner and outer self; intellect and emotion; conscious and unconscious. Enjoy seeing extraordinariness in the ordinary. OK. So I'm an optimist.

Steve Waling

I've been writing poetry since I was asked to write one for the school magazine. I don't think I write to 'change the world' so much as to see it clearly, as if for the first time. I don't have any big messages for anyone, I'm not trying to make a point, I'm just trying to point at things and say, 'look at that!' Afterwards, you can make your own mind up about if it means anything.

Jan Whalen

I constantly scribble things in notebooks then try and fit them together to make poetry. For me, a successful poem communicates my experiences to people in a way that delights rather than scares them. Even if that experience is the back end of a city with not a daffodil in sight.

Rosanna Imogen Wright
Poetry is of the moment. It must tell a story which not only I can access. I try to write poetry on subjects which many people can empathise with, whilst still reflecting on my own experiences. I enjoy writing poetry because it is cathartic and it allows me to have my voice heard.